Enduring the Process

My Faith vs Breast Cancer

by
Na'Tasha Moore

ISBN: 978-0-578-66042-4

Enduring the Process

Proudly self-published through Divine Legacy Publishing, www.divinelegacypublishing.com

Acknowledgements

To My Children
Ra'mon and Zoey, I love you dearly. There are no words that can express the love I have for my heartbeats! Thank you for being along side of me every step of the way, caring for me, making sure I had what was needed, calling on your breaks to check on me, you were there. But most of all I want to thank you for being strong for me and honoring my wishes. I'm so proud to be your mother.

To My Mother
Mom, thank you. I needed you and you were there, day and night sitting with me, never leaving me alone. I'm thankful for you and dad and all that you do. I know it wasn't easy on you, watching your only child go through this, but your strength and encouraging words touched me deeply. I love you.

To My Pop
Thank you for encouraging me to be strong,.I know this was hard for you; I could see it on your face. I'm thankful for you and Ma for being there.

To Shuntell

My bestie, I will start by thanking you for being there! You were with me through the tests, the diagnosis, taking me to every appointment, keeping me calm, finishing my sentences, and asking questions when I would forget or become angry. You had my back. You allowed me to react. And told me it was okay, and that God would take care of me. Your prayers, and your presence through it all and still now, are truly appreciated. I'm so thankful for you.

To Jackie

My dear friend, thank you for your prayers and your loving support. You used to have this saying, "Although we do not talk everyday and we may not see each other often, but one thing for certain is that our friendship would always remain the same picking up wherever we left off." I called and you came to see about me. Thank you! I'm thankful for our friendship of many years.

To The Fathers of My Children

Thank you for everything! You stepped in and took care of things without any hesitations and helped your children while I was recovering. God bless you both. My heart is filled with so much gratitude.

To Jay

Thank you for your love for me and relieving me of the stresses that go along with medical expenses. I'm so appreciative of you making sure I got the best care possible. Blessings to you for all you do.

To My Mentor/Spiritual Mother

Rosemary Daniels, you have been such a blessing in my life. I am so grateful for your love, your prayers, and support. You have been such a positive influence in my life as I faced many obstacles along my journey, including my fight against breast cancer. Love you. Thank you!

To My First True Love World Outreach Ministries Church Family

I want to thank you for your prayers and all the calls to check in on me while I recovered. I appreciate you all.

To My Ochsner Family

Team registration, management and coworkers, thank you for your support.

To all others whom I may not have mentioned, thank you for your prayers and support...

Letter of Encouragement To My Readers

Our dreams, goals, and inspirations should begin with boldness and great confidence as it has power and creative productivity in it.

In all processes of life we are faced with challenges, some more so than others as it affects us all differently. As a breast cancer survivor it has been my experience that my focus wasn't geared toward the breast cancer in which I was enduring, but how I chose to handle it. In all things, whether good or bad, I made the choice to rely on my unwavering faith, depending and standing firmly on the words of God. I realized having a negative mindset will never give you a positive outcome in life.

We may have endured storms that have changed our lives, but learning to love yourself and adjust what's needed to live your lives is a healthy place to start. You do not have to allow what you've endured to change who God created you to be. You can choose to live and fight with everything in you. Your life is worth fighting for....

Process 1
My Life As It Was

My life as it was in the summer of August 2017 was what I considered to be a normal life. I was healthy and actively enjoying life. The only health issue I had was my fluctuating blood pressure, which I had been managing with a prescription.

I was a loving mother of two amazing children whom I adored. I was excited about my life and even more so excited about the important events in my children's lives that were quickly approaching: My daughter was graduating from the Aveda Institute, a Cosmetology school in a nearby city in September 2017 and my son was getting married to his high school sweetheart the following September 2018.

I never really was big on having a large group of friends to hang out with. My idea of a great weekend consisted of shopping with my daughter or meeting my "Girls Gone Wild" senior edition crew Shuntell and Charlene, whom I'd been close with for over 26 years. We'd go for drinks at one of our favorite restaurants or we would take a forty-five minute drive to New Orleans to Bourbon Street to Club Razzoo's where the atmosphere made us feel like we were 25 again. Yeah we wished, but there is nothing wrong with living in fantasy every now and again. I don't recall ever not having fun when we went there.

Life was good, and I couldn't have been more pleased with how things were going for my family and I, not to mention I had decided to go back to school to finish getting my degree in social work with a concentration in counseling. I'd been working on completing my degree for what seemed to be forever, but life always happened and then, of course, it happened again. Nevertheless, although trials in life somehow always found their way to me, I still strove for completion despite life's ups and downs. I thought if I were to become successful in achieving my degree, it would allow me to develop more and become more resourceful in my abilities to help people. Since I've been on this journey one of the things I've come to realize is that you do not have to possess a degree to have compassion for people while assisting, informing, inspiring, or encouraging people. This is who I am! God had already given me what I needed, and everything else would fall into place all in God's timing.

I smile thinking about my love for people and how I am wowed at the many conversations I have had with numerous people, never fully understanding what made me so inviting and trustworthy to talk too. Since starting my journey I can honestly say, now I know. I laugh as I think of the times my daughter Zoey and I were on outings or at the grocery store and she would always look at me and say, "Momma we can't go anywhere without you talking to people." Or my best friend Shuntell staring at me from her counter, smiling and shaking her head as I talked with customers on a daily basis, which in some cases lasted for more than just a transaction of things being bought. It turns out they both were right! No matter where I went, I always knew someone or had random conversations with people I would encounter. I believe that I have been walking towards my purpose in life the entire time.

Although I was going back to school and that would result in a career change, I worked for a great hospital organization where I adored my job. I worked as a Patient Access Representative, where I provided check in services for patients, entering their information and verifying insurances upon checking them in for their scheduled appointments. Surprisingly, there were many amazing conversations that took place at check-in. My job allowed me to interact with people on many different levels, and some of my encounters would turn into fostered relationships. This had become a part of who I was since I could remember; something about it just felt right. No matter how big or small, it has always been immensely important to me to be a blessing to others.. I just wanted to make a difference or put a smile on someone's face. I cannot express enough about the joy I feel when I am doing so. All for the Glory of God. Because I've worked in the medical field for over 25 years now I have become more aware, more knowledgeable, and more resourceful, therefore I will not hesitate to apply myself wherever I am needed to assist people in need.

I can remember talking to my children often as they were maturing into young adults about taking care of themselves, being informed, and getting yearly checkups. I made sure they understood how important it was for them to do so, while setting examples for them as they witnessed me taking care of myself over the years. I was one of those people who never skipped a yearly exam, and if I thought anything was wrong in between time, I would make an appointment. One thing we must remember is often times we can do all the things we feel are right or that we are supposed to do, and things can still happen in our lives. This very thing happened to me, which led me to share with you, my readers, my story/testimony.

I believe that sometimes God will allow us to go through things in our lives when our focus isn't where it should be or we may need to just be still and trust in Him and stop trying to fix things ourselves by forcing matters on our own. I can only speak from my own experiences of such actions taken. I rely on what I've learned throughout this process, and I no longer force things to my own understandings. I trust God and, no matter what the situation or test may be, He is in control. "And we know that all things work together for good to those that love God to those who are called according to His purpose" (Romans 8:28).

If we just believe in God's promises to us, and stand on his word, we would in my opinion, gracefully endure all processes in life.

Process 2
Intuitions and Discernments

I have always felt the gift of having keen perception and intuition even as a young adult in my late teens, early twenties. It scared me at first; no one expects to think or have a vision of something and shortly after, it happens or comes to pass. Therefore, I had to seek spiritual guidance to better my understanding of the many intuitions I was experiencing. I know this probably sounds a bit crazy, so I will give you an example of what I'm talking about.

One summer my daughter and I were driving along the interstate heading to Alabama for the weekend. I'd taken my SUV to be serviced before we left, so all was well for traveling. I can remember having feelings of what I thought were anxieties about traveling, but shortly after the feeling, or intuition, I passed a car on the side of the road with a flat tire. I didn't think too much of it, and I proceeded on. I passed another person on the side of the road fixing a flat tire. I said to myself "these roads are hot, everyone is having flats today" not knowing what I was in for.

We always stopped at the same rest area when traveling to Alabama, so we were to be there in about another 5 miles. As we continued on, there was an 18 wheeler behind us. It appeared as if he was trying to get my attention flashing lights, and I could hear the horn blow several times. I thought I was driving too slow and was in his way so I moved into the other lane, and he continued on but still was blowing his horn. The exit for the rest area was approaching so I told my daughter "we are going to take a break and let the truck go on". I thought the driver was having road rage, but little did I know he must have seen something wrong with my tire that I couldn't. Once we stopped, for some reason I circled my truck looking at the tires and I even looked under the hood. There was no visible sign that anything was wrong.

When we got ready to continue our drive, something within me said, check the front tires again, so I did. There was one tire I went directly to, which was on the driver's side. I touched the tire, looked at the tire a couple times, and still I did not see anything wrong, not even the smell of rubber. We left and got back on the interstate. You will never guess what I saw on the side of the road? Yes! Another vehicle on the side of the road on flat! It was two miles later I had a horrible blow out! It was that same tire that I touched several times at the rest area. This blow out could have taken our lives. It was just that bad. My daughter and I are very thankful for God's protection, and the team of registered nurses who was in front of us and pulled over to help. The image is still fresh in my memory, as they ran to help us.

I can tell you now that all the signs were there, although they were visible to me. I could not recognize what it all meant until I had a clear understanding of having intuitions and discernments. I had no clue, but now since I have sought spiritual guidance I understand when something is being shown to me immediately, without conscious reasoning, and recognizing when it is God speaking to me, discernments. Every believer is born with it, but not everyone will recognize it. I can tell you, my readers, it has been a journey of spiritual growth, both mentally and physically. So now that I have given you an example of one of my many experiences, I will continue on with my reason for sharing this with you.

Before I was diagnosed with Stage Two Invasive Ductal Carcinoma Breast Cancer, I can honestly say that there were warning signs which led me to speak to team members at my job about some questions I had, which led me to having diagnostic testing done. I was forty-four at the time. When it came to my yearly exams, I was always on time; needless to say for the last four years that I had my mammograms done the results were always negative for any signs of breast cancer. The results would always coincide with the physician's readings of having dense tissue and caffeine knots. I was told this was normal, nothing to worry about. I don't like to think about what would have happened if I would have trusted the results from the mammograms.

It was my intuition of events, signs, and inner feelings that led me to become active in getting the proper testing. I would get phone calls from organizations who were involved in breast cancer research all through the day and night. These calls always left me feeling as though I was being prompted or warned. It's hard to explain. All I know is that I was alert to every call. I was also moved to another department at my job where they specialize in women's health, including mammogram testing. I was beginning to encounter women who were experiencing the same illness I unknowingly would be facing. I often wondered whether I was getting placed in position for something that was to come, not thinking it would be me that would be enduring breast cancer. I have learned while enduring this process that we must be our own advocate when it comes to our healthcare. I'm not saying that we should take matters into our own hands; what I am saying is be informed, do your research, and know your body. If something feels wrong, then it's worth looking into. The body gives us signs, whether its an unusual ache, rash, swelling, or change in shape. We just have to be aware and be able to recognize what's normal and what is not.

I took into consideration all the warning signs I had experienced. The thoughts of these events stayed with me, causing me to become even more aware of what my body was already telling me. I can't speak for anyone else, but for me when something becomes consistent, recurring in my mind, I begin to pay close attention to it. There is absolutely nothing wrong with being proactive when it comes to our health. I would much rather know about anything involving my health early on than later. So I say to you my readers, listen to your inner being, that gut feeling that's deep within. It's a gift, God's gift of intuition. I am speaking from a place of experience. I am in no way claiming to know all, but I can speak from all of what I have endured as it has affected me during this process. I'm thankful, blessed for being able to recognize when God is speaking to me, and grateful for understanding the many intuitions along the way.

Process 3
The Exam

It was August 2017. The time for my annual breast exam was near. I always seemed to have some sort of anxiety about my exams especially when I just had an intuition that something was wrong. I had faithfully checked my breasts every month as we are encouraged to do, and to feel something that's doesn't feel normal was scary. I just couldn't wrap my mind around what I felt to be just "dense tissue" as I had been told previously for my yearly mammograms. I mean, I had symptoms of swelling, redness, soreness, and I could actually feel the lumps in my left breast while examining myself while showering. The symptoms were painful and my breasts would become heavy and hot to touch, especially around the week before my menstrual cycle.

I knew when I scheduled my appointment this time, I wanted answers. I did not want to hear anything about it was normal, it's hormonal, or from drinking coffee or other caffeinated drinks. As I mentioned earlier, I worked for a hospital clinic in the women's center where mammograms and other gynecological care was given. I had spoken to my coworker Angela who worked as a technician in the mammography department. I'd asked her questions about the symptoms I'd been having, and she immediately advised me to call my primary care doctor to inform him of my concerns and request that he give me orders for a diagnostic exam. Immediately I sent my doctor a message with my concerns and without hesitation my doctor put the orders in for the diagnostic testing that same week. My coworker, Angela, who works in the mammography department had apparently seen the orders and remembered our previous conversation about my results of all my previous exams and came to me saying she had a 1:30 appointment for me that day. I declined because I'm a private person and wanted to schedule at another location for testing, but she did not give up, saying "1:30 Ms. Tasha" and walked off. Needless to say, I went to the appointment Angela had scheduled.

The diagnostic exam began, and I had a strange feeling. As I looked at Angela, I could tell by the look on her face that she saw something that was alarming. My reaction was calm. I can remember saying to her, "it's not just dense tissue, is it?" She never replied, only telling me to stay positive and she was going to call the radiology department to get me worked in for an ultrasound. I was a nervous wreck! My thoughts were all over the place, filled with anxiety about what I would find out. I went to the appointment down in the radiology department and had the ultrasound done. The technician was very thorough, and she scanned a particular area on my left breast several times. This would be the side the cancer was later found on. I was told by the technician that I would be notified about my results in a few days.

I was nervous all day, wondering and contemplating about what they had seen during the ultrasound. Meanwhile at home I tried my best to stay calm, but my family sensed something was wrong with me because of my behavior. I found myself quiet and distant, as I was deep in thought. I don't remember getting any sleep that night as I saw every passing hour on the clock. The next day around noon, I got the call. The ultrasound had found 2 masses in my left breast, one 2.5cm and the other a little over 3cm. They now wanted to schedule a biopsy for the following week. Although I was frightened by the urgency in the technician's voice, I did schedule the next available appointment. I just wanted to get this over with. I needed to know what I was up against.

The radiologist told me it would take a few days to receive the results back from the biopsy. I was not anticipating the wait time at all. I told myself that everything was going to be okay, easier said than done. I was an emotional wreck. I had to figure out a way to keep myself busy so that I would not have time to think of all the things that could possibly go wrong.

Several days had passed. It was a Friday afternoon, and my daughter, Zoey, decided she would hang out with me while I ran some errands. I felt like she knew something was wrong with me and wanted to stay close. While we were out, I decided to stop in at the bank to open another account. Zoey decided she would sit in the car and listen to music while I was in the bank. My phone rang, and I immediately told the teller excuse me I needed to take the call as I noticed it was the number from my doctor's office. It was the nurse calling. I thought she was calling to tell me to come to the office for my results, but instead she told me over the phone that what the biopsy showed was in fact breast cancer and I needed to come into the office.

I was so upset at the poor way in which this was delivered that my hands were shaking, and I could not get a word out clearly! I just said "Okay" and hung the phone up as I stood there in front of the teller in tears. The teller began to ask me if I was okay. I replied, I was not expecting to be told I had breast cancer over the phone. I could see the compassion in the teller's eyes as she looked with disbelief. My mind immediately focused on my daughter who was in the car waiting for me. I had to get it together before getting into the car. The teller offered me a tissue and water and called me into a room down a short hallway to have a seat. I sat there for a few minutes, trying to process what I'd just been told the best I could. I just did not want to upset my daughter by telling her the diagnosis. Once I calmed down, I spoke with the teller and explained I would have to finish at a later time. She understood and wished me well as I left the room.

When I got back into the car, Zoey looked at me and asked, "Momma are you okay?" I responded, "yes baby I'm okay, not feeling to good suddenly," trying to cover up what had been told to me. I then asked her if she could call her friend Tyrielle to go shopping with her, as she and I had planned to do once we left the bank. I just needed some alone time to process things. I drove straight home from the bank, and Zoey, still looking a bit confused, left shortly after we arrived to meet her friend. I began to deal with what I'd been told. The breast cancer diagnosis.

Process 4
Coping with the Diagnosis

As I looked around my home, I couldn't help but stare at the pictures on the mantle of my beautiful family. Suddenly, I began to scream with anger and then fell to the floor, uncontrollably crying out to God, asking, "Why me Lord?" The spiritual person that I am would never in my conscious mind question God in any way. Clearly that day I was not myself. Everyone and everything that was important in my life weighed on my mind heavily. It was almost like I gained ten pounds with the thoughts swirling through my mind.

My children faces flashed in my mind, and all I could think about was how my children needed me.

Question after question rotated in my brain: Who would be there for them as I am? Who would love them and nurture them as I do? Who would help them, encourage, and support their dreams as I always have? Nobody. And for that very reason, I knew one thing and one thing for certain: I had to fight! I could not allow breast cancer to take me away from my children. I was beyond disbelief. I could not stop the tears from falling, just sitting there thinking about all the what ifs of my life, my children, my family.

Eventually I had to find the strength to tell someone. I reached over to the sofa that was nearby, grabbed my cell phone, and immediately called my mother, Dinah. Of course, I'm sure you can imagine, my mother quickly became upset and frantic of what could possibly be going on as I tried my best to get the words out to inform her of my diagnosis. Instead I became speechless. I froze up when I tried to speak, all I could do was scream and this was followed by me crying out to my mother. For her, as she sat on the other end of the phone, I imagine it was like dealing with a newborn baby crying, in need of her mother's care and the only way to make her mother aware of the severity of her need was to cry out. As my mother screamed into the phone in a panic asking me, "Tasha! Tasha! What's wrong? Are you hurt!? Baby talk to me!" my reply was nothing more than a cry for my mother. My mother then screamed with pain and anxiety in her voice. "I'm on my way," she said before abruptly hanging up the phone.

My mother lived several miles away from me, but it was approximately 10 minutes later and my mother was knocking with distress at my door. The door was unlocked; I had not locked the door from Zoey leaving earlier so she rushed right in. And there on the floor is where she found me. She screamed at the top of her lungs for my stepfather to come as she didn't know what was going on. She immediately fell to the floor where I was kneeling, still in disbelief, embracing me into her arms and asking me, "Tasha what's wrong?" I remember looking up at her and her eyes filled with tears as she had never seen me in this way. I muffled out to her, "They told me I have breast cancer." I felt her compress her feelings, trying to be strong for me, but I could see the fear in her eyes as she tried to comfort me. She told me that everything was going to be okay, that we were going to get through this together. My stepfather, Johnny, came over to us embraced us both, comforting us as we all were in disbelief.

Once my mother and I were able to calm down, I began to tell her all that I had been going through. I gave her a more in-depth perspective about all the tests and stress I had been dealing with. Up until this point, I had not disclosed this life changing information to anyone other than my best friend Shuntell. I am a very private person, and I will also admit to thinking I could handle this alone. What I've come to realize is that even the strongest individuals need help-- someone they can turn to. I have always been the one that everyone, even strangers, felt free to share their innermost feelings, problems, and situations with. Well, this time I needed a support system that I could turn to and depend on. At this moment it became clear to me, I could not handle any of this alone.

I decided not to tell my daughter until after she graduated from the Aveda Institute, which was to take place within the next week. I didn't want to distract her from her schoolwork; she had worked so hard and come so far, I knew this would only distract her from reaching her goal. I decided to call my son Ra'mon over to the house while Zoey was at school and talk to him about my diagnosis. Ra'mon had just moved out and was beginning his new life with his future bride Christina. This was going to be very difficult for me and for my son. I am very close to my children, so I dreaded seeing the fear in my son's eyes when I shared with him the diagnosis I'd been given.

I asked God to give me the strength not to breakdown in front of him because it would be devastating for him to see me like that, as he has never seen his mother in a vulnerable state. After all, my children thought of me as their superwoman: A woman of great strength and endurance, always pushing through any obstacle that got in my way or the way of my children. I had to get myself together. I had never faced anything as hard, or as terrifying, as having to tell my children that their mother was in for the fight of her life against breast cancer. I did not know what to expect from him; I just prayed to God that he would be able to handle it.

Ra'mon arrived later that afternoon once he had gotten off from work. I was there waiting for him. I had the strangest feeling that he already knew something was terribly wrong with me from the way he greeted me. It wasn't our normal playful way of greeting each other, and I could feel the tension in the room, the nervousness in his hug as he embraced me saying

"Hey Momma, how are you?"

I replied, "I've been better Son."

I politely asked him to have a seat next to me, and then I begin to tell him the diagnosis. He sat quietly for a moment and, as his eyes begin to fill with tears, I embraced my son. "I am going to fight with everything in me. We must keep our faith in God, and he will guide us through this," I said. If you can imagine being hit unexpectedly in the stomach and having the wind knocked out of your body, this perfectly explains what I felt, along with the pain of seeing the fear in my son's eyes and the shaking of his trembling hands as I held him close to me made it worse. I just remember praying and asking God to strengthen my children and prepare them for what was to come. Once we gathered ourselves, I told him that we could not tell his sister until after her graduation. We both agreed that was best, with all that I had going on. I didn't want it to affect Zoey's moment; I wanted her to fully enjoy her moment. This was something she had worked very hard for, and we would just deal with telling her afterwards.

The next few weeks would be busy as I planned for my battle with this beast. They were filled with appointments as I searched for the best team of providers to begin my fight against breast cancer. I went to work that week and notified my management team to file the necessary paperwork to take a leave of absence, and I am so thankful for my Ochsner family. My managers, Ericka and Jannifer, assisted me every step of the way and also helped with finding my team of providers. My team lead at the time, Kirklin, made sure my shifts were covered for all my appointments and leave time. The support I received from my coworkers was awesome. God placed me amongst an amazing group of people and to all of them I am forever thankful.

On September 9th, my Zoey was graduating, and my emotions were all over the place. It was a mixture of being happy, I was so proud of her accomplishments, as well as a feeling of sadness weighing in on my heart because I couldn't keep this news from her any longer. I couldn't imagine her thinking she was left out of the loop, and I didn't know what to expect from her. She was my baby. "Lord help me!" was all I could think.

We got through the ceremony and planned a dinner together with her cousin Stephanie, who was graduating as well. It was a beautiful time watching her in that moment, and it was amazing to see her enjoy her accomplishments and the time she spent mingling with her family and friends. She stayed over her friend's house that night so they could continue their celebration. I was relieved that Ra'mon already knew, because I don't think I could have told her alone. I asked him to come to the house the next day once Zoey made it in.

The next day, sometime that afternoon Zoey made it home and Ra'mon arrived shortly afterwards. It was time to tell my baby. I called her into the living room where her brother and I were seated. As always, when I wanted to talk to them together, I would say, "okay we're having a family meeting." This was my way of getting their attention, and usually it was always of importance when we had family meetings. I began to talk to her about what I had been going through and the diagnosis the doctors had given me. She looked at me with disbelief, bursting into tears. I reached over to comfort her, but she was afraid for her mother and angry wanting to know why was this happening. She stormed out, going to her room. This was heartbreaking, to see my daughter in so much pain and there was nothing I could do about it except promise her I would fight with all my being and for her to trust in God, the same as what I had told my son. I was an emotional wreck as Ra'mon rushed to his sister's room to comfort her, hoping to calm her down. After a while, I no longer heard her crying. I was so happy he was there to help comfort his sister while she dealt with what she'd been told. This was in fact the hardest thing I'd ever had to do.

Process 5
The Breakdown

Breakdown: A non-medical term used to describe an acute, temporary, short phase of a disorder with features of depression or anxiety.

My days became distant and my nights were even farther away from the people I loved. This was in fact the most difficult process, but I felt it was very necessary to go through all the different feelings and emotions. I later realized the very same emotions allowed me to go through the steps to survive breast cancer. I hated feeling angry and lashing out at my loved ones. There is absolutely no way I could have gone through this without reacting, or even feeling guilty, as I did, but I later realized it was okay to feel guilty. We are human and we react to how we feel emotionally. I would sometimes take a weekend trip to be alone so that I could react and cry out. As strange as it may seem, it helped. I didn't have to be strong at my most vulnerable time. I never wanted my children or my family to see that side of me.

This was my absolute lowest point of enduring. I just could not wrap my mind around what was happening to me. I thought since everyone close to me had been told of my diagnosis it would be easier to deal with. I was wrong! I told myself that I would not allow this beast to affect me mentally. I was wrong again. What I had discovered was the fact that it was already affecting my mind. I began to lose sleep as I was up all night thinking and pondering the devastating thoughts in my mind. Of course, this wasn't healthy for me, or anyone else who has ever had to face cancer or any other life altering illness. I became easily irritated at the least little thing that wasn't done right or maybe it was and I just took what was going on with me out on everyone around me.

It seemed that I deceived myself into thinking that I was okay. I was everything but okay! I was angry and could not believe this was happening to me. We never know how we will feel when we are faced with illness or obstacles in life until it's staring us face to face. I was emotional and afraid of all the things that could possibly go wrong. This wasn't me at all! I was always the strong one. This in fact made matters worse. I vaguely remember having thoughts about medical and life insurance, whether or not I had enough and would my children be strong enough to take care of things or did I need to appoint someone to help them if things went badly for me. I was all over the place. One thought to the next. I was becoming mentally exhausted. I often wondered if this was what people meant by the saying "I saw my life flash before my eyes" when something terrible would happen to threaten their life. If it wasn't, it surely was how I was feeling, one thought after another.

One day I decided to speak to my son about some of my anxieties about the what if's and the things that could possibly go wrong. This talk did not go well at all. He was upset and said these words to me, "Who is this person, and where is my mother, my superwoman?! You're talking like you're giving up Ma! This isn't you at all!" he screamed, scolding me like my grandmother use to when I would say a bad word. This hit me hard, like a ton of bricks. I really had to get myself together.

Because breast cancer affects us all differently, there isn't a right or a wrong way of dealing with it. It was my experience receiving a cancer diagnosis brought on different emotions, anxieties, and without a doubt fear of uncertainty about life itself and how we would survive this beast and live with the outcome. As a result of discovering and admitting that I was having difficulty accepting the diagnosis given to me, I began to rely even more on my faith and what I felt deep within about the power of God. I knew that I had to trust my process in it all if I was going to get through this. I'm thankful for the support and spiritual guidance of my mentor through it all. I honestly felt as if God was speaking through her. I always felt a sense of calmness after she and I would talk. I also had to allow my children and my family to see me and all the vulnerabilities that I was enduring so they would understand how to comfort and support me through this.

Needless to say, because I went through different emotions of endurance, I changed my mindset and focused on what I believed and not so much about the emotions of it all. By doing so, I no longer felt angry nor did I feel depressed. I somehow felt empowered, strong, and fearless. Yes! I was given the diagnosis of Stage 2 Ductal Carcinoma Breast Cancer, yes it would change my life forever, but I did not have to allow it to change who I was or what I believed in. I began to feel better, more positive, and even somehow empowered about my fight against this beast, breast cancer.

Process 6
My Family's Love for Their Superwoman

I never imagined in my wildest dreams that I would have experienced the things that I have experienced with breast cancer. Since diagnosed, I experienced the different emotions of anger, anxieties, and pain on different levels of intensity. In reality, no one is happy about going through such an experience but, for me, it was very necessary for my acceptance of the breast cancer diagnosis as well as my reactions, especially towards my family. Often times, we won't allow our family to see our vulnerabilities or the things that frighten us the most. In all honesty, not only was I afraid of what was happening, I also was afraid for my children, my family, and what this would do to them. I never thought about my actions, not talking to them about my feelings or allowing them to be support-ive and comforting to me. This was just as painful for them as it was for me, and it affected them tre-mendously. My family loved me; I knew this without a reasonable doubt. It appears I had for-gotten about the power of love and the strength in it, how a family's love never ends. I needed my children, and my family and they needed me.

After realizing how much I needed my family and they needed me, this process began. I will ad-vise anyone to have a talk with family members about the do's and don'ts while going through any illnesses, especially cancer and the treatments to follow. As I've expressed before, it affects us all differently. For me, if I was having a bad day and wanted to be alone, they respected that but checked on me throughout the day. My children would come home from work on their lunch hour in addi-tion to calling. I didn't feel as helpless or vulnerable as I did in the beginning. I was no longer angry. What I have learned about myself in all that I have endured is the fact that I do not like to be depend-ent on anyone for anything; it makes me feel helpless somehow. I know right! Everyone needs someone at some point in their lives.

It took getting diagnosed with breast cancer for reality to hit me in the face. I mean literally hit me like a ton of bricks! I won't say it didn't take time getting used to all the attention my family was giving me, but I was sure happy they were there. I remember waking up 10/17/17 from having my first surgery, a double mastectomy with reconstruction to follow, and seeing my family's faces waiting for me in my room. There were no tears, only warm smiles as they greeted me with hugs and kisses and comforting words of encouragement. I thought to myself, this is love. I could feel it and it was an amazing feeling. It's okay to be strong and independent, but never lose sight of your family's love for you and their willingness to help in time of need. After all, I had been there to take care of my family, and now it was time for me to allow them to do the same for me. It didn't mean that I was no longer the superwoman of the family. It meant that I could no longer do all that I was doing, like maintaining the house, running errands, doing the laundry, making meals and such things, and it was time for me to trust in them and their abilities to step in and take care of it all.

It doesn't hurt to talk about it. Understanding and communication is an important factor in the giving and receiving, without feeling guilty. I almost allowed my guilt and feeling the need to hide my vulnerabilities to make me miss out on my family's love. I had to realize part of the anger I felt had nothing to do with my family; it was all me because I felt like I was losing my role in the family and my independence was being taken away from me, but it was neither. They were trying to be just what I needed: a support system while dealing with this very traumatizing ordeal. Support is very important to have while dealing with this beast of cancer and any other illnesses, trials, or the terrible hands we are dealt in life. We all need an outlet, someone to be there. So why not your family? It still amazes me how much I have learned about myself, the good and the bad, while fighting for my life. No one is perfect. We fight to live and for me I rely heavily, wholeheartedly on my faith in God that I can do all things through Christ who strengthens me (Philippians 4:13), including beating the beast, breast cancer.

Process 7
Faith Over Fear: My Testimony of God's Healing

It was October 10, 2017. I will never forget this day for as long as I live. I can remember coming home from work and deciding to go to the revival being held at my place of worship. I'd been anticipating the event all week. As I began to get ready to attend the event, I was approached with a conversation that quickly turned into an unexpected argument, but knowing what I know now, it was definitely meant to be a distraction. I was very upset about what had taken place, and my first thought was that there is no way I'm going to church looking like this, make up was scattered and my eyes were red from crying! I decided I would just go to bed. I then laid across my bed, and shortly after I had laid there something came over me and stayed on my mind. I thought to myself, "get up" I will not allow what has upset me to keep me from going to hear the words of God.

I can remember getting up so fast that I became a little dizzy. I got up and got myself together and made it to revival on time. Reflecting on what had taken place, I know now that it was God talking to me (discernment) telling me not allow myself to become bothered by what was meant to distract me and keep me away from Him. I needed to push through and proceed on with my day. My dear readers, I am so thankful for the spiritual growth along this journey. If I had allowed the argument to distract me from attending, I would have missed what God had in store for me. I will begin.

On that night my church home, First True Love World Outreach Ministries, had a Pastor by the name of Antoine Headspeth to speak. The spirit was definitely in the building as worshiping began and proceeded on. I was happy, my spirits were lifted, and I just kept saying to myself "Thank you Jesus I made it". The congregation began to settle down for the visiting pastor to begin his sermon, or as I like to call it, his teaching or lesson. I was in deep thought about my health. My ears and heart were open to every word as Pastor Headspeth poured out the words of God.

There was an altar call to release anything that may have been troubling us or anything that we wanted to leave there, giving it all to God. While standing at the altar there were many different things going on such as praying, etc. Then there was a silent moment from Pastor Antoine Headspeth. He stopped in the middle of what he was delivering to the congregation. He said, "God just put something in my spirit!" I heard him clearly, I was there, front and center! I can remember my hands were up in worship and my eyes were closed as I sought the closeness of God's presence.

He then said, "There is one, one person here tonight with cancer. God said he is about to heal you of this cancer. Are you here?" I can remember feeling frozen, as if I wanted to open my eyes and mouth and say something but for some reason I couldn't! He made the call again, "Are you here? If you are here and cannot speak, wave your hands!" At that moment I could feel my arms and hands swaying, and in that instant Pastor Headspeth was in front of me asking me, "Sister is that you?" My eyes opened with tears flowing down my face. I answered, yes! He repeated asking me again, "Sister is this you?" My response was yes again.

Pastor Headspeth then said to me, "God is about to heal you of this cancer. Do you believe it?? I answered, yes! I remember him praying in great detail, speaking in tongues, and asking for the congregation to lift their hands toward me as well in prayer. Pastor Headspeth walked back over towards me, still in prayer about the healing that God had placed in his spirit, and as he approached me he touched my forehead. Please allow me to pause. I don't know about you, but for me I often wondered about the laying of hands and the Holy Spirit. Growing up Baptist, I've seen it and my older relatives talked about it all the time, but never had I experienced it to know how it felt. I'll continue. I had a feeling come over me that I can't really explain to this day.

Once Pastor Headspeth touched my forehead, my body became very light and I began to shiver as if I was cold, but I wasn't. I tried to control the shaking of my arms and legs, but I had no control over what was happening to me, and yes, I fell out on the floor, crying out, trembling, and shaking out of control. I had never felt what I was feeling, never in my life! I know now I was experiencing God's presence and God's healing of my body through the Holy Spirit. While trying to get myself together I could see a blur of fellow church members around me, one in particular was Sis Rosemary Daniels, who had been like a mother, a mentor, an inspiration to me for some time now. I could see her moving rather quickly kneeling to the floor beside me. As she kneeled, she placed her arms around me, lifted my head, rocked me into the comfort of her arms, and said to me, "Daughter I knew it. I knew God was gonna heal you" and she began to praise God.

As revival went on, I was still in shock at what I had just experienced. When it ended, I remember walking fast to my car, only to burst into tears again, tears of joy of course, thanking my Savior for healing my body and just feeling thankful. I was grateful for God's anointing that I was able to discern God's voice and ignore the negativity that had taken place earlier that day that could have distracted me, causing me not to receive what God presented to Pastor Headspeth to deliver to me. When I arrived at home, Ra'mon and Zoey were home waiting for me, not knowing what I'd experienced. They witnessed something in my behavior that something had definitely happened as I paced the floor. I was still in tears praising God and thanking him for my healing, his grace, and his mercy over my life. This went on for the next 2 hours, as I was still in worship.

Once I was able to settle down, I begin to talk to my children as they had a look of fear on their faces. I finally spoke out to them saying, "I'm okay, just give me a moment and I will explain." I told them about my experience, my healing that had taken place, and how I felt differently somehow! They looked at me wide eyed and in disbelief as they hugged me, asking continuously if I was okay. As time went on, it became very visible to them what I'd told them. My entire thought process was different. I can speak boldly about what I endured. My life as I knew it had not been the same. My faith was stronger than ever, unwavering. I trusted God wholeheartedly. I was healed; it was already done. I just had to "Endure the Process".

I remember having a conversation with my team of doctors, the oncologist, the surgeon, and plastic surgeon prior to the revival at my church. My oncologist and surgeon had informed me of everything that was due to happen moving forward, his recommendations, the dosage and how long I would need chemo and radiation, and the possible side effects of it all. Of course, at that time, all the information was a bit overwhelming, but I listened and I prayed about what I had been told. I called on my church mother Sister Rosemary and other prayer warriors for support as well. I am a firm believer that there is power in prayer! I can remember praying after that visit, asking God to give me ease of all treatments, if I had to have any at all. I stuck it in my Bible. In my mind, I had given my request to God, and I left it there.

The following week, October 17, 2017, I was scheduled for surgery. I was to have a double mastectomy, which is the removal of both breasts. The diagnosis of breast cancer was only in my left breast, but due to the facts of the genetic testing which showed me to be a carrier for the hereditary gene I made a conscious decision to remove them both. I can remember having a meeting with Sis Rosemary at our place of worship. She and I went to her office and she prayed with me. Once we were done, she gave me a document of healing scriptures that was prepared for individuals going through illnesses, such as myself. She told me to read them every day and to meditate on God's word and his promises. I did just that. This was the first thing I did after thanking God for allowing me to see another day every morning and it was the last thing I did before I closed my eyes at night. This had become my routine, and anytime I felt weakened by negative thoughts of this beast I was fighting, I would read them again and meditate on God's words. I felt strong and empowered some-how, I was not wavering in my faith! You see, I had put my trust in God and what He said in his words. I understood that I was to listen to the instructions the doctors had given me, so I prayed for them as well, that God would guide them in providing my care as well as successful surgeries. I had even asked the doctors before making the decision that they would be my team if they believe in God. Thankfully, they replied "Yes!" because I did not want anyone who did not believe in God a part of my team. Needless to say, they are still today apart of my team.

I arrived for surgery 10/17/2018 at 5:30am, my healing scriptures in hand. Of course I was nerv-ous, all kinds of thoughts were racing through my mind. I began to read and one particular scripture stayed with me: "Fear is not of God. Rebuke it." (2 Tim 1:7 NKJV).

I began to repeat this over and over to myself until I became calm. My faith was stronger than ever and although I believed I was completely healed of breast cancer, I knew I still had to go through my process, so I checked into the hospital and the process began.

The nurses began to prep me for surgery. Once everything was signed and the IV was started, I could see the concern on my family's faces as they comforted me, assuring me everything was going to be okay. I'd asked my children to allow me to check and began before coming. I did not want to see the fear in my children's eyes. I knew this would have cause problems for me going into surgery. But I knew they would be there waiting for me when it was over.

Six hours later, after surgery, I awakened to a nurse looking down over me with these bright blue eyes smiling deliriously. I remembered looking into those same blue eyes before the medicine put me to sleep. I nervously commented to the nurse that "When I wake up I want to see your face and those pretty blues." The nurse smiled and she assured me she would be right there. She kept her word.

Once I was stable, they moved me to my room where I was greeted by my wonderful family! I was so happy to see my children and the rest of my family. I became overwhelmed with emotion; we all were emotional. As I lay there and the medication began to wear off, I noticed that I wasn't in any harsh pain. It was mostly soreness across my chest and underarm where they removed lymph nodes to test whether or not the cancer had spread. It was later determined that it hadn't spread, and I didn't need chemo or radiation. I can boldly say prayer works. It changes things and it will definitely bring you through any situation. I prayed for ease in all that I had to endure with breast cancer. I believed; I did not waver in my faith. I trusted in God and his words and things I prayed for were coming to pass. God is faithful.

Process 8
Life-Altering Decisions

I was always told that life was about the choices and decisions we made. Never in a million years did I ever think I would be making decisions about whether or not to remove my breasts in order to have a better chance at beating cancer. After all, I think it's fair to say that they were trying to kill me! Part of me wanted to just keep them, and do whatever was medically requested of me. Then once I really thought about it, after speaking to my team of physicians about the diagnosis, prognosis at hand, and what they intended to do about it, it was suddenly became clearer to me what I needed to do for me.

They asked me questions about my family's history and whether breast cancer was common in my family. I knew neither my mother nor her mother had experienced cancer of any kind. Other than that, I knew nothing about my family's history. This is one reason why it's extremely important to know your family's history of any illnesses. Because I didn't know, the doctors recommended I get a genetic screening done. The genetic screening is a testing, which is done by a blood sample. This test screens, diagnoses, and identifies carriers for genetic disease determining whether patients have a hereditary gene to a disease. There is so much information out there. Although I received a booklet on the genetic testing, I still did my own research on line. Two sites in particular I visited a lot were myriadwomenshealth.com and mysupport360.com. I found then to be very informative, but by all means be your own advocate regarding information, your healthcare, and what's right for you and your process.

With all the information I had acquired both from doctors as well as my own research on this testing, I was definitely in agreement with them to have this test done. I have children, and I would want them to know If I was a carrier for the gene mentioned and I am so happy I did. Turned out I was positive for the hereditary gene mutation. It was common somewhere down my family tree, I just wasn't aware of it. I felt like a load of bricks were suddenly placed on my shoulders when I was given this news. When it comes to my own health that's one thing, now the fact that I carry the gene, my children will have to be tested as well. As a mother I never want my children to have to experience not even a fraction of what I have while fighting this beast! I discussed the test and its findings with my children and close relatives and asked that they at some point get tested. Of course this was a shocker for them too because we had no knowledge of this running in our family. I felt like this was another missing piece to a puzzle or something.

Shortly after I discussed the results with my family, it amazed me that no one had anything to say other than to do what I felt was necessary and best for myself. I appreciated this so much from my family. This was one less thing I didn't have to stress about.

The following day I scheduled an appointment with my team of doctors to give them the decision I made concerning my treatment options. The oncologist and surgeon recommended that I had the surgery first since it appeared from test results that they could remove my affected left breast safely. I must admit, the genetic screening helped me tremendously in making the decision to remove not just the affected left breast, but both breasts with reconstruction to follow. My team of doctors discussed and counseled me for over an hour about my decision to remove both breasts, as they only wanted to remove the affected one. In their minds

I was still young and judging from my personality they did not feel that I would be able to cope with being breastless. I was getting frustrated as they pushed and pressured me trying to get me see things their way. That was not about to happen! I finally told my team of providers in a much authoritative tone that, "My breast was never my biggest asset, instead it was my thick legs and nice butt that was!" I can laugh about saying that now, but at the time I was not! The look on their faces once I said that told me they knew I was serious about my decision and there was no changing my mind. As difficult as I thought it was going to be for me making this decision, it wasn't. The more I learned about my diagnosis and began to understand the information that was given to me by my team of doctors, my decisions became a little easier, less frustrating. I was ready. I wanted to evict this cancer from my body as soon as possible. These were my exact words to my team. Get it out! Now, no wasting anymore time.

October 17, 2017 was the day I would say goodbye to my girls and evict this beast of a cancer from my body. I prayed, prayed, and then I prayed some more. I read my set of healing scriptures day in and day out. I was calm and ready to evict this cancer from my body. I knew in my spirit, in my heart, that God had healed my body already. This was the kind of faith I had. I just had to go through the process, and this was it.

My family was there, as the nurse prepped me for surgery, with positive thoughts and prayers as they were preparing to roll me back to the operating room. You got this! We will see you when you come out. It really touched my heart to see the strength of my family's faces. They were doing just as I asked them to do: be strong for me and pray. As they were rolling me into the operating room, a pair of sky blue eyes looking down at me and a soft voice calling my name is all I heard and saw before the lights went out. Needless to say, surgery was a success. They were able to remove both breasts with no spreading of the cancer. My team of doctors were also able to place the tissue expanders for my reconstruction with no complications, and strange as it may seem I had no pain, just soreness. That's all God. I was surviving! This was a constant thought in my mind: I can do this, now I just need to stay strong and focus on my healing and the reconstruction.

My recovery from having the mastectomy and reconstruction was going well for the most part up until a month later in November 2017. I began to run a fever, which caused me to go to the doctor and from there I was admitted to the hospital with high grade fever. My body was rejecting the tissue expanders, causing an infection. I thought to myself "Here I go again!" Just when I think I'm doing well, something else surfaces causing more issues from this beast. What I thought was going to be a great success turned out to be more decision making. What was going to happen now? I prayed, prayed, and prayed some more! This was my answer for every obstacle that surfaced.

After my oncologist and plastic surgeon cleared me of the infection, the surgeon wanted to remove the expander on the affected side, which was my left side, same as where the cancer was and continue to build the right breast. Of course, this did not make any sense to me. It was just too much for me to handle at that point. Of course the pressure was on again from my team of doctors for me to only remove what was needed and continue to build my right breast and start over with the left breast once it was healed. I prayed about it, and rehearsed what I had been through since being diagnosed over and over in my head like a broken record. I came to a conclusion and decided I'd had enough! I didn't care what they said, and frankly I didn't want to hear anything about it; I just wanted them to do what I asked.

The next day when my plastic surgeon made his rounds, he stopped in my room to update me on blood work from the previous day. I begin to tell him that I had decided to remove all reconstruction, not just the affected one. He tried to talk me out of it, telling me that I was young and I would probably miss having my breasts, all of which I'd heard before from the same surgeon during my first surgery. Sure, I thought about what my surgeon said to me, I'm human, but my thoughts and answer remained the same as before. I was okay with not having breasts! I meant what I said early on about my breasts not being a big asset to me! Or did he forget? Yeah, I know how crazy it may seem for a woman to just rule out having breasts, but in my mind they literally tried to kill me, so why would I try to keep building them knowing that I carry the hereditary gene. In all honesty, it's how I felt about it, and I was tired of defending my decision to my team of doctors. It was final, the decision was made! Another eviction.

Because I was already admitted in the hospital for the infection, instead of releasing me, we decided to schedule the surgery to remove the reconstruction the next morning. To me this was like having another double mastectomy. The surgeon removed both tissue expanders and reconstruction work that had been done during the first mastectomy. I was relieved, the surgery went well, and the soreness was controllable with regular Tylenol. Again, that's all God! I felt so blessed to have gone through two major surgeries a month apart successfully with little to no pain, but how could I expect to be in pain when I prayed and asked God for his grace and mercy? I believed in what I prayed for, and it came to pass. This process was one to reckon with, trying to make the best decisions for myself so that I could do the best I could with picking up the pieces of my life and moving forward. I really believe that once I determined my breasts did not define me, I was ready to do whatever I had to do to survive. I just wanted to

live and continue to enjoy my children as they began to build their lives and start their own families.
I'm so happy I chose me, my needs, what works for
me in my life, and not what everyone else thought
was best for me. Flat and fabulous I will remain...

Process 9
Recovery and Self-Doubt

"Who am I?" was the question that filled my mind with uncertainty. I wasn't sure anymore after all I'd been through with the mastectomy and failed reconstruction. I knew without a doubt that feeling the way I did wasn't due to me losing my breasts. I was comfortable with making that decision. Something else seemed to be missing. It was definitely time to find myself as well as my new norm, whatever that was! Feeling this way, all I knew was that I had to find it and quick. I did not like the indescribable feelings I was having. It was mind-boggling. The more I thought about it, I was missing.

During my process, my fight with the beast, I tried my best to remain confident in who I was from the very beginning. It didn't matter what I was being told by doctors about not being the same as before breast cancer, vibrant and full of life as I was and appeared to them. For some reason my team of doctors felt the need to remind me that there would be no cleavage for sundresses, swim-suits, or even low-cut blouses by removing my breasts and not replacing them with reconstruction. They were so sure I would have a problem with this. I even had to deal with some of my relatives and friends telling me how they felt I would feel incomplete, even possibly depressed, without my girls. It angered me as I heard them suggest all the things that I could possibly go through while fighting and making decisions for my life, but it didn't matter. I continued to tell myself that I would not allow the breast cancer, or the physical changes I had to make, to change the woman God created me to be.

Needless to say, I still questioned myself, asking will I ever be the same? We are human, and we are not by any means perfect. In my opinion, it's okay to question if you are not sure about something. I realized that there is no wrong way, question, or action taken when fighting for your life. We have to do what's best for us at that very moment of any uncertainty. In this life, we make choices, we grow from them, and we make changes, hopefully all for the better. If you fail, or do not exceed your expectations, don't lose hope, nor faith or your confidence. Gather yourself and try again! This is what I found myself doing while going through this process.

Often times I would go off to myself and just think of my life before the diagnosis, the person, the woman I was. I thought about all the things I had endured some good, some bad. The people I have encountered, some I'm still very close with, others I am no longer associated with. All due to choices, but my life continued, so what made this any different! It was a diagnosis, I didn't have to give up living, I had to fight to continue living my life! It amazes me how when something drastic or life altering happens in our lives we tend to think about all the things that should, would, and could have been. What I've discovered in my process of recovering and having doubts about myself and life moving forward, is not to allow influences of others, illnesses, or even the influences of this world dictate or persuade you away from knowing who you are as a person and what is best for you. Yes, we endure things in life. Yes, unfortunately we encounter illnesses and different conditions that can sometimes affect our way of living, but we are still who we are. I'm sure everyone won't feel the same as I do, and that's okay.

We are all affected differently and we react differently. I'm speaking from my place of endurance as this happened to me. I experienced these things while trying to recover from all that breast cancer brought into my life as well as what it's taken from me. This is a day to day process, as other things surface. For most of us, we receive the treatment recommended, we go through the surgeries, we take the meds they prescribe us to take, we deal with the side effects of hair loss, nausea, fatigue, mood swings, depression, headaches, shortness of breath, weakness, tingling or numbness, swelling of parts of our bodies, difficulty speaking and understanding, vision problems dizziness, and weight gain. Yes! I can honestly say that I have and still experience all but 3 of these side effects. This by no means was easy to come to terms with, but it's my life and I was willing to do what I had to do to continue living it. Because I experienced side effects from treatment, I began to realize that all the things I love to do were being affected by the side effects I was experiencing. If I was going to be honest with myself and not only fight for my life but my way of living, I was definitely going to have to make some changes. I began to find my new norm after breast cancer.

Life as we know it is full of unpredictable changes; sometimes we just don't realize it until something happens. I, for one, was not expecting to have to alter how I'd always done things I was so accustomed to doing, and might I add doing them my way! As challenging as it was, I began to find and embrace all the changes I had to make in order for me to continue living my life as close to normal as I possibly could.

Being the organized person that I am, I chose to start with the things I needed to alter that affected my health. This meant I had to clean up my eating habits, including less sugar in my diet and staying hydrated. Of course this, for me, was the hardest, but it's a part of the process. My hair and vision changed drastically after I began to take the oral medication Tamoxifen, so this caused me to make an appointment with the ophthalmologist. I now have glasses. Because I already wore short pixie cuts for my hairstyle, I decided to cut them shorter due to the thinning of my hair. Moving on to the next thing, I then had to make the decision as to whether or not I would wear the prosthetics, or "foobs" as some survivors or people who have encountered breast cancer like to call them, or would I change the types of tops I would wear. I decided I would do both, depending on the clothing and how it fit. This was an easy fix for me being that I am so versatile.

The most difficult change for me during this process of finding my new norm was my shoes. I loved my heels, tall boots, and wedges. Unfortunately, I am still working on this change. If you are a shoe lover you probably understand why I'm still working on it. I have had to change from a stiletto heel to a block heel, from tall to 1 to 2 inch boots or wedges. I disclosed the changes I had to make as an example of doing what was needed to live my life and do the things I enjoyed comfortably. I knew my joints would not allow me to wear the heels I was accustomed to wearing, so I changed them. I wanted my clothing to look as fashionable as it looked before, so I altered the way I wore it. I think you get the point I'm trying to make. All of these changes were to help me adjust my life and make things work for me. Not changing who I was as a person, but allowing me to find my new norm after my battle with the beast breast cancer. So who am I? I am Na'Tasha Moore, a mother, breast cancer survivor, and author who has decided to fight for my life and embrace the changes that are necessary for my survival and way of living.

Process 10
Getting
Back to Me

As a 45-year-old recently divorced cancer survivor, I've had my reservations about what was considered to be the norm for my new lifestyle. I always thought of myself as being confident, vibrant, and full of life. Once you have encountered breast cancer, things suddenly don't feel the same or look the same. You will have to excuse me as I may be a little transparent in my discussion about this process. Once I was discharged from the hospital, after having both breasts removed, I suddenly found myself feeling depressed, feeling unattractive, and not feeling whole. I tried to put it out of my mind, and embrace the fact that I still had life. I would give myself these pep talks day in and day out, hoping that somehow they would change the way I was feeling about myself, but they didn't. I can remember getting dressed and undressed and not even looking in the mirror until I had put on my shirt. This was very odd, being that I loved looking at myself in the mirror while getting dressed. I guess one could say I loved my body and the way it complimented my clothing, some would probably say clothing complimented my body, but I meant it just how I said it.

Once my oncologist and breast surgeon gave me the "okay", that my healing process had gone well and the incisions from both surgeries had healed, I could slowly resume my normal activities. Well, that was exactly what I was trying to figure out! What activities would I resume? I was scared out of my mind. What was normal? All I knew was I absolutely loved life, and I wanted to continue doing all things I had planned for myself, including dating. Who doesn't want companionship? Of course, there were many doubts going through my mind, wondering if I would feel sexy or what would a man really think about dating a breastless woman. I had all these questions and emotions runny through my head as I really began to process the whole recovery stage and the fact that I had endured and survived breast cancer. What I began to realize while going through this process was that I am still a woman! There are no ifs, ands, or buts about it. I may have been through what I've been through and I may have to change the way I do some things, but in my mind I'd decided that I would not allow the after effects of breast cancer stop me from being who I was before. I promised myself from that moment on I would love me as a whole and not deprive myself of anything, and I would not allow myself to be afraid of meeting new people. I'd be open to dating and experiencing new things like traveling, after all we are supposed to live our absolute best life. I believe this is when self-awareness kicks in, believing in yourself and knowing your strengths and capabilities not allowing fear to set in, after all "Fear is not of God" (2 Tim 1:7NKJV). Once I realized all these things, I was ready to live what was now my norm.

Moving Forward

I had been conversing on social media for a while, interacting, sharing my story, my testimony with individuals about my cancer journey with hopes of inspiring anyone who would read it or listen to what I had to say. While doing so I was also meeting new people. It's amazing how you never know who knows who or even who may be related when you are meeting people, especially on social media.

It wasn't long after postings that I had gotten the attention of a young man on one of my pages. Ironically, I had been observant to him as well, go figure! He and I began conversing back and forth for a couple of months. The more we talked, the more something was feeling a little familiar to me, including his last name, so I inquired about who he may have been related to. It turns out he was the son of one of my customers from a previous job, whom I still have a close relationship with. I was floored! I really did not know what to think, so I decided to speak with her, letting her know that I had met one of her sons. It was a Friday after-noon, and I decided to give her a call to tell her the news. She was excited that we had met! Long story short, he and I planned our first date in the nearby city of Hammond shortly after that.

The Date

This young man, who I now refer to as John Coffee, was amazing! Not only was he handsome, he was respectful and attentive. Still feeling a little reserved, I felt the need to have a conversation with him about my diagnosis and a little of what it entailed. I know for some this probably would be a little too soon, but for me and my mind set I want-ed to be very upfront and honest about my situation with whomever I allowed into my person-al space. Sometimes you must step out on faith and do what you feel is right for you and your best in-terests at the time. There is no right or wrong in this! Life is about the choices we make, I agree, but who would know better than self as to when it would be appropriate to have this conversation. Right! I always tell people because I absolutely des-pise dishonesty! I'd much rather be honest upfront, giving the individual the opportunity to decide for themselves whether or not they would like to continue moving forward.

As I was speaking, John Coffee smiled and stopped me, singing these words to me, "You are so beautiful to me" melting my heart of course. He then told me that he understood I had been through a life-altering event and he understood my concerns, but I needed not be concerned. This man told me that he admired my strength and my courage, he only wanted to keep a smile on my face, and that having a mastectomy does not alter what he sees when he looks at me. As you all can imagine, I was full of emotion and speechless. I finally gathered myself and muttered the words "thank you." He then said to me, "Suga, (what he called me) I see Coretta Scott King, Michelle Obama strength when I look at you! You are strong, you are beautiful and full of life. I have nothing but respect for you." Of course, that put me in my feelings to be compared to such great women who have made such an impact on our lives today. I was lifted, tremendously! I cannot express it enough! All the anxieties of dating went away, the concerns I had about being breastless were no more!

As we continued dating and spending time, the intimate factor tipped into our relationship. I can honestly say John Coffee and I had chemistry that was so strong it was unreal! What we shared was so passionate and full of love! The intimacy he had given me was different on so many different levels, and it was nothing that I had experienced before. Let me be clear, I am not speaking of just sex! Intimacy is much more than that. He had given me all that I needed to feel like the woman I'd questioned being early on, post mastectomy.

I shared this very personal story with you, my readers, as it is my intent and my hope that I encourage you to love yourself first, and don't be afraid to pick up the pieces, experience new things, date, or meet new people. Discover what will work for you and your new norm. My way of finding my norm will not be the next person's way, and some may not agree to what I am saying, but this is my story as it happened. This is what I experienced while going through my process of recovering. I'm not saying things will be perfect, or that you may not run into trials along the way, but at least try and if you don't succeed then you try again. We are not perfect, and we are going to make mistakes along the way. What matters is that we learn from them, recover, and keep it moving! Yes we may have endured some effects of breast cancer, but we still have to love ourselves enough to fight for our lives and live, embracing our scars and any other changes to our physical being that we may have while going through our process. Although these things have happened to us, we are still who we are. We have to have faith in God and trust our instincts and intuitions about life and people with hopes that when the time is right we will find our norm and possibly meet that special someone who will see us for who we really are as a person and as a woman!

I appreciated all the compassion this man showed me. Although the first step was loving self, I will always acknowledge the significant role John Coffee played in my life during my recovery process. It doesn't matter to me that we didn't move forward into a long lasting relationship. I honestly don't think that was the purpose of he and I crossing paths. I'm a firm believer that sometimes people enter our lives for a reason and a season, sometimes just passing through as they are only there to complete a specific assignment and move on. Ironically, we both recognized that, and we were there to help and comfort one another in that specific timing. There were a lot of things that never crossed my mind until I met this young man; one thing comes to mind as I am writing is that sometimes the simplest things in life can be the best things in life. This is a true statement. In the world we live in it's so easy to get caught up in "the stuff" or the lack thereof that we forget how to enjoy one another while exploring our hopes, dreams, and inspirations. That's a thought to ponder. In closing, what I appreciate more than anything from this experience with John Coffee was that we have built an amazing friendship that will last a lifetime, promising to always be there for one er! Never will I forget "Snoopville."

In addition to this very important process of getting back to me, I felt that it was very important for my readers to know the male perspective on the very same process in response to being asked about our relationship and how he felt about meeting and dating me, a survivor of breast cancer. I want my readers, as well as survivors and other women who may have had to remove or alter their breasts in any way as I did, to know that you are still the person you were before the change. We just have to adjust things, embrace the changes made, and continue to push forward living our lives. I'm not saying it's not emotional or discouraging. We are not only human as I have said earlier on, we are emotional by nature. Deciding to move forward with dating was very important to me and I made the choice to be honest and trust that there were men out there who would be supportive, compassionate, and loving towards me and other women who have come against this life altering beast, breast cancer regardless of them having breasts or not. In fact, I found men to be even more attracted to me and my strength of endurance while I was fighting for my life and now even after I've survived. This was encouraging.

John Coffee's Perspective

The question was asked, "What was your experience meeting and later dating Tasha?" and this is what Mr. John Coffee had to say:

Life is a process. It's also about learning new things and meeting new people. For me, I met this one special lady by the name of Tasha. She caught my eye on social media. As I would scan through her pictures I would always say to myself, man this is a beautiful lady. It was just something about her, she had that glow. I reached out to her one day and unexpectedly she answered back rather faster than I thought she would. We started conversing and come to find out she was a friend of my mom's. That just shows you how God works!

We ended up exchanging phone numbers and talking on the phone for a few weeks. Then, after chatting, we ended up meeting up for lunch one day in Hammond, LA at a nice restaurant. From the first time I saw her I just thought she was a beautiful woman. We sat down and got comfortable. As we talked, just her conversation and how professional she carried herself turned me on. She seemed like a very strong black woman. The more I sat and talked to her she reminded me of Coretta Scott King with the classiness of Michelle Obama.

In the middle of lunch she told me, there's something I want to tell you. She said, "I want to be honest and upfront with you. She grabbed both my hands and said, I am a cancer survivor! I lost both breasts to cancer." She then said, "I want you to know this before we move on or things get any deeper." I was so in love with how beautiful she was, how she talked and carried herself, the breast cancer and her not having breasts was not going to be a problem for me. I told her we can work around that, it's not a problem. She seemed like, after that point, she was one of the happiest woman on God's green earth.

We began dating and seeing each other more often. I like to call her Tasha Moe, but I can tell she didn't like that name, so I started to call her my "Suga". That really made her smile. She was the perfect queen for a perfect king. In a physical form, your spine is your support for the body and that's what she was to me! Now that's deep! As we dated more, we became closer, intimate. I knew through our conversation that this was going to be a process with her being comfortable being around me topless. But to me she was so beautiful, inside and out, that didn't matter. I just wanted her to be comfortable at all times around me. I could see she was determined to not let breast cancer keep her from being comfortable as far as dating and going back to living a normal life. That was real powerful to me, along with the way she was straight forward with me from the beginning to the end about her being breastless and sharing so much information with me about breast cancer.

This was new for me, but I just loved her company so much that I really overlooked her cancer situation and being breastless. I think that's what made our relationship so special. I also think that her going through this and meeting someone who easily accepted her situation made her have more belief and self esteem in just being the woman that she once was before breast cancer. Every time we would meet up on the weekends, her face would have that glow like she was filled with so much positive energy. That made me feel so good knowing that she was genuinely happy with herself and life.

I started telling her she was my Bonnie and I'm your Clyde. That really made her smile. She nicknamed me "John Coffee." I learned so much from her, just watching how proactive she was. The way she had stepped out on faith, creating her own platform, helping and talking to other women that are going through the same situation that she is. I also realized it was the simplest little things that made her smile, like me singing a few lines to the only song that I knew: "You Are So Beautiful, To Me". She is a blessing in my life, seeing how strong she is from losing both breasts to going through the oral treatment prescribed, its side effects, and still standing strong. An amazing woman, single parent of a son and daughter who has been her rock and support system. Sometimes God sends those special ones into our lives whether it's for a few seconds, a few weeks, a few months or a lifetime. But I knew whether we were in a relationship or not, our friendship would last a lifetime. Forever she would have that title of being my Bonnie and I, her Clyde.

My Life Now as a Survivor

My life now, as a survivor of breast cancer, is more about me living my absolute best blessed life. I promised myself I would not be afraid to live my life because of all the unknowns that come with breast cancer. For example, will it come back? I decided I wouldn't live in fear! Of course, I will be attentive to follow-up appointments and do as my team of physicians advises me. When a life-altering event takes place in your life, it really makes you very aware of what's important and what's not! I see things very differently than I did before. I now have a bucket list of things I want to do and places I would love to visit. Although traveling is new to me, it feels great stepping out of my comfort zone and planning to take trips. There is so much we deprive ourselves from experiencing due to fear. When I really think about my life, sometimes it saddens me that it took me to encounter the beast and become a survivor of breast cancer to realize I had not even begun to live my life. I cannot make up for lost time, but it's never too late to start. Love self first, and love the life you live. Blessings.

Scriptures of Great Faith . . .

These scriptures were given to me in my time of need by a woman of God, a minister from my church home. Then, ironically, these very same scriptures were given to me again while I was recovering in the hospital after surgery in the same order they were given previously. This really spoke to me spiritually and encouraged me even more to trust God as I endured my process. They gave me comfort and peace, as well as helped to strengthen my faith, believing in God's words and promises to us. These scriptures have become apart of my life as I meditate daily reflecting on how, through having faith of a mustard seed, I began to believe that with God nothing is impossible to overcome.

These scriptures were significant as I struggled to gather myself from all the anxieties, emotions, and uncertainties about my life after the diagnosis. I knew I had to stay focused and keep the words of God present in my being if I was going to get through this. In these scriptures, I was relieved knowing that God's words would not fail.

When I was diagnosed, I listened to the doctors and all they recommended for treatment and so forth. These given scriptures encouraged me to pray continuously day in and day out and meditate on God's word and His promises to us. I prayed, asking to be healed. As I shared in process seven, I expressed how God's words did not fail and all that I prayed for came to pass. What a feeling! It really is a feeling like no other to have experienced God's presence and His healing!

These scriptures brought about awareness within myself, as they reflect on all the different processes of my journey while fighting against breast cancer. As a believer of our God, I felt a deep sense of gratitude. It became very clear to me that my journey wasn't just about surviving breast cancer; it was about connecting spiritually with God and building a relationship with my Father. As a believer, I kept my faith in God who sustains me speaking, praying, believing that because we live in the Spirit of God, and He raised Jesus from the dead, He will do the same for all who are in Christ when that time comes. It gave me peace. I will bless the Lord at all times, serving God selflessly without complaints, instead with great appreciation for God's grace and mercy over my life and all that He does.

I get excited at the very mentioning of our Lord and Savior. Often times I sit in my quiet space and think about all the times God's grace and His mercy kept me, and how God has blessed my life over and over again even when I did not deserve it. I'm so thankful for God's love for us. My thought process may be different from yours and that's okay.

The things we endure in life affect us all differently. We respond in different ways.

It is my intention to encourage you to never give up, no matter what you are faced with. God has given us life and where there is life there is hope and where there is hope there is strength of endurance.

May your hearts be blessed.

The word of God will save your life...

My son, give attention to my words; incline your ear to my sayings. Do not let them depart from your eyes; keep them in the midst of your heart. For they are life to those who find them, and health to all their flesh. (Prov 4:20-22 NKJV)

Your Thoughts:

God's word will not fail...

Not a word failed of any good thing which the LORD had spoken to the house of Israel. All came to pass. (Josh 21:45 NKJV)

Your Thoughts:

God's will, healing, is working in you...

For it is GOD who works in you both to will and to do for His good pleasure. (Phil 2:13 NKJV)

Your Thoughts:

The spirit of life is making your body alive...

But if the Spirit of Him who raised Jesus from the dead dwells in you, He who raised Christ from the dead will also give life to your mortal bodies through His Spirit who dwells in you. (Rom 8:11 NKJV)

Your Thoughts:

God is for you...

For all the promises of GOD in Him are Yes, and in Him Amen, to the Glory of GOD through us. (2 Cor 1:20 NKJV)

Your Thoughts:

It is God's will for you to be healed...

And behold, a leper came and worshipped Him, saying, Lord, if You are willing, you can make me clean. Then Jesus put out His hand and touched him, saying, "I am willing; be cleansed." Immediately his leprosy was cleansed. (Mat 8:2-3NKJV)

Your Thoughts:

Obey God's word and be healed...

And said, "If you diligently heed the voice of the LORD your GOD and do what is right in His sight, give ear to His commandments and keep all His statutes, I will put none of the diseases on you which I have brought on the Egyptians. For I am the LORD who heals you." (Exo 15:26 NKJV)

Your Thoughts:

Serve the Lord and healing with be yours...

So You shall serve the LORD your GOD, and He will bless your bread and your water. And I will take sickness away from the midst of you. (Exo 23:25 NKJV)

Your Thoughts:

God takes all sickness away from you...

And the LORD will take away from you all sickness, and will afflict you with none of the terrible diseases of Egypt which you have known, but will lay them on all those who hate you. (Deu. 7:15 NKJV)

Your Thoughts:

Obey all God's commandments and receive all His blessings...

Bring all the tithes into the storehouse, that there may be food in My house, and try Me now in this. "Says the LORD of hosts, "If I will not open for you the windows of heaven and pour out for you such blessings that there will not be room enough to receive it. (Mal 3:10 NKJV)

Your Thoughts:

One of God's benefits is healing...

Bless the LORD, O my soul; And all that is within me, bless his holy name. Bless the LORD, O my soul, and forget not all his benefits: who forgives all your iniquities, who heals all your diseases, who redeems your life from destruction, who crowns you with loving kindness and tender mercies, who satisfies your mouth with good things, so that your youth is renewed like the eagles. (Psa. 103:1-5 NKJV)

Your Thoughts:

God's word is healing...

He sent His word and healed them, and delivered them from their destructions. (Psa. 107:20NKJV)

Your Thoughts:

God wants you to live...

I shall not die, but live, and declare the works of the LORD. (Psa. 118:17 NKJV)

Your Thoughts:

Choose to live. Be a fighter...

I call heaven and earth as witnesses today against you, that I have set before you life and death, blessing and cursing; therefore choose life, that both you and your descendants may live. (Deu. 30:19NKJV)

Your Thoughts:

You will live a long life...

With long life I will satisfy Him, and Show him My Salvation. (Psa. 91:16 NKJV)

Your Thoughts:

Jesus bore your sins and your sicknesses...

But He was wounded for our transgressions, He was bruised for our iniquities; The chastisement for our peace was upon Him, and by His stripes we are healed. (Isa. 53:5 NKJV)

Your Thoughts:

God will restore your health...

For I will restore health to you and heal you of your wounds, says the LORD, because they called you an outcast saying: "This is Zion; No one seeks her." (Jer. 30:17 NKJV)

Your Thoughts:

*You can take authority over
the sickness in your body...*

Assuredly, I say to you, whatever you bind on earth will be bound in heaven, and whatever you loose on earth will be loosed in heaven. (Matt. 18:18 NKJV)

Your Thoughts:

Agree with someone for your healing...

Again, I say to you that if two of you agree on earth concerning anything that they ask, it will be done for them by My Father in heaven. (Matt. 18:19NKJV)

Your Thoughts:

What you say will make a difference...

So JESUS answered and said to them, "Have faith in GOD." For assuredly, I say to you, whoever says to this mountain, 'be removed and be cast into the sea,' and does not doubt in his heart, but believes that those things he says will be done, he will have whatever he says. (Mark 11:22-23 NKJV)

Your Thoughts:

Believe, and you will receive...

Therefore I say to you, whatever things you ask when you pray, believe that you receive them, and you will have them. (Mark 11:24 NKJV)

Your Thoughts:

Plead your case to God...

Even I am He who blots out your transgressions for My own sake; And I will not remember your sins. Put Me in remembrance; Let us contend together; state your case, that you may be acquitted. (Isa. 43:25-26 NKJV)

Your Thoughts:

Have someone lay hands on you for healing...

And these signs will follow those who believe: In My name they will cast out demons; they will speak with new tongues; They will take up serpents; and if they drink anything deadly, it will by no means hurt them; they will lay hands on the sick, and they will recover. (Mark 16:17-18 NKJV)

Your Thoughts:

Worship God...

Now we know that GOD does not hear sinners; but if anyone is a worshiper of GOD and does His will, He hears them. (John 9:31 NKJV)

Your Thoughts:

The devil wants to kill you;
God wants to heal you...

The thief does not come except to steal, and to kill, and to destroy. I have come that they may have life, and that they may have it more abundantly. (John 10:10 NKJV)

Your Thoughts:

You are redeemed from the curse...

Christ has redeemed us from the curse of the law, having become a curse for us (for it is written, "Cursed is everyone who hangs on a tree), that the blessing of Abraham might come upon the Gentiles in Christ Jesus, that we might receive the promise of the Spirit through Faith. (Gal. 3:13-14 NKJV)

Your Thoughts:

You will not waver in your faith...

Let us hold fast the confession of our hope without wavering, for He who promised is faithful. (Heb 10:23 NKJV)

Your Thoughts:

You can have confidence in GOD and His word...

Therefore do not cast away your confidence, which has great reward. (Heb. 10:35 NKJV)

Your Thoughts:

You can find strength in
GOD and His word...

Let the weak say, 'I am strong'. (Joel 3:10 NKJV)

Your Thoughts:

Jesus Christ has never has never changed.
What He did in the Bible,
He will do for you today.

Jesus Christ is the same yesterday, today, and forever. (Heb. 13:8 NKJV)

Your Thoughts:

God's highest wish is for you to be well...

Beloved, I wish above all things that thou mayest prosper and bi in health, even as thy soul prospereth. (3 John 1:2 NKJV)

Your Thoughts:

Be anointed with oil by a Christian who believes in healing...

Is anyone among you sick? Let him call for the elders of the church, and let them pray over him, anointing him with oil in the name of the LORD. And the prayer of faith will save the sick, and the LORD will raise him up. And if he has committed sins, he will be forgiven. (James 5:14-15 NKJV)

Your Thoughts:

Jesus has already paid the price for your healing...

Who Himself bore our sins in His own sins in His own Body on the tree, that having died to sins, might live for righteousness; by whose stripes you were healed. (1 Pet 2:24 NKJV)

Your Thoughts:

Be confident in your prayers...

Now this is the confidence that we have in Him, that if we ask anything according to his will, He hears us. And if we know that He hears us, whatever we ask, we know that we have the petitions that we have asked of Him. (1 John 5:14-15 NKJV)

Your Thoughts:

God answers the prayers of those that keep His commandments.

Beloved, if our heart does not condemn us, we have confidence toward GOD. And whatever we ask we receive from Him, because we keep his commandments and do those things that are pleasing in His sight. (1 John 3:21-22 NKJV)

Your Thoughts:

Fear is not of God rebuke it!

For GOD has not given us a spirit of fear, but of power and of love and of sound mind. (2 Tim 1:7 NKJV)

Your Thoughts:

Cast down those thoughts and imaginations that don't line up with the word of GOD.

For the weapons of our warfare are not carnal but mighty in God for pulling down strongholds, casting down arguments and every high thing that exalts itself against the knowledge of GOD, bringing every thought into captivity to the obedience of Christ. (2 Cor 10:4-5 NKJV)

Your Thoughts:

Be strong in the Lord's power. Put on His armor to fight for healing...

Finally, my brethren, be strong in the Lord and in the power of His might. Put on the whole armor of GOD, that you may be able to stand against the wiles of the devil. For we do not wrestle against flesh and blood, but against principalities, against powers, against the rulers of the darkness of this age, against spiritual hosts of wickedness in the heavenly places. Therefore take up the whole armor of GOD, that you may be able to withstand in the evil day, and having done all, to stand. Stand therefore, having girded your waist with truth, having put on the breastplate of righteousness, and having shod your feet with the preparation of the gospel of peace; above all, taking the shield of faith with which you will be able to quench all the fiery darts of the wicked one. And take the helmet of salvation, and the sword of the Spirit, which is the word of GOD; (Eph 6:10-17 NKJV)

Your Thoughts:

Give testimony of your healing...

And they overcame him by the blood of the Lamb and by the word of their testimony, and they did not love their lives to the death. (Rev 12:11 NKJV)

Your Thoughts:

Your sickness will leave and not come back again...

What do you conspire against the LORD? He will make an utter end of it. Affliction will not rise up a second time. (Nahum 1:9 NKJV)

Your Thoughts:

Connect with the Author

Email: authornatashamoore@gmail.com

Facebook: Author Na'Tasha Moore

Instagram: @author_natasha_moore

Creative Control With Self-Publishing

Divine Legacy Publishing provides authors with the guid-ance necessary to take creative control of their work through self-publishing. We provide:

Writing Coaching

Professional Editing

Author Branding

Self-Publishing Coaching

Graphic Design

Website Design

Let Divine Legacy Publishing help you master the business of self-publishing.